Let Freedom Ring

Harriet Tubman

by Nancy J. Nielsen

Consultant:
Xiomara Santamarina, Assistant Professor
Center for Afroamerican and African Studies/Department
of English
University of Michigan
Ann Arbor, Michigan

Bridgestone Books
an imprint of Capstone Press
Mankato, Minnesota

Bridgestone Books are published by Capstone Press,
1710 Roe Crest Drive, North Mankato, Minnesota 56003.
www.capstonepub.com

Library of Congress Cataloging-in-Publication Data
Nielsen, Nancy J.
  Harriet Tubman / by Nancy J. Nielsen.
    p. cm. — (Let freedom ring)
  Includes bibliographical references and index.
  Summary: A biography of the African American woman best known for her work with the
Underground Railroad, describing her childhood as a slave, her escape to the North, her
assistance to the Union during the Civil War, and her accomplishments during the
Reconstruction years in helping former slaves adapt to freedom.
    ISBN-10: 0-7368-1087-0 (hardcover)   ISBN-13: 978-0-7368-1087-6 (hardcover)
    ISBN-10: 0-7368-4523-2 (paperback)   ISBN-13: 978-0-7368-4523-6 (paperback)
    1. Tubman, Harriet, 1820?–1913—Juvenile literature. 2. Slaves—United States—
Biography—Juvenile literature. 3. African American women—Biography—Juvenile literature.
4. African Americans—Biography—Juvenile literature. 5. Underground railroad—Juvenile
literature. [1. Tubman, Harriet, 1820?–1913. 2. Slaves. 3. African Americans—Biography.
4. Women—Biography. 5. Underground railroad.] I. Title. II. Series.
E444.T82 N54 2002
305.5'67'092—dc21   2001005000

Editorial Credits

Charles Pederson, editor; Kia Bielke, cover designer, interior layout designer, and illustrator;
Jo Miller, photo researcher

Photo Credits

Cover: Hulton Getty/Archive Photos; CORBIS, 5, 6, 17, 23, 32; North Wind Pictures, 7, 9
(top), 11, 12 (large), 14, 19, 21, 27, 42; PhotoDisc, Inc., 9 (bottom), 30, 39 (small); Artville,
LLC, 12 (small photos); Hulton/Archive Photos, 24, 35, 37, 41; Stock Montage, Inc., 31; Lee
Snider/CORBIS, 39 (large), 43

Special thanks to Robin Blake for research assistance.

Printed in the United States of America in Eau Claire, Wisconsin.
042014
008166R

Table of Contents

Chapter One

General Tubman

A group of slaves had been waiting for the right time to escape. One night, they heard cannon shots coming from the nearby river. Three Northern gunboats were coming.

Instead of running from the boats, the slaves picked up their possessions and raced toward them. The slaves were about to become free. The soldiers on the gunboats lifted bombs from the Combahee River and plowed ahead. The soldiers shot at enemy soldiers, bombed a bridge, and helped nearly 800 African Americans to freedom.

This scene happened in 1863 on South Carolina's Combahee River. The U.S. Civil War (1861–1865) was raging. In charge of the mission was a woman named Harriet Tubman. Along with

Harriet Tubman (above) earned the respect of many people. She led hundreds of slaves to safety and served the North in the U.S. Civil War.

Colonel James Montgomery, she commanded 150
African American soldiers, members of the Union
Army from the North. Though Harriet was not a
member of the army, the men respected her. They
called her "General Tubman."

Harriet Tubman was famous for leading many
slaves to freedom before the Civil War. Few people,
however, know about her role during the Civil War.
She worked as a nurse, a scout, and a spy. Without
her help, expeditions such as the Combahee Raid
would not have been possible.

$100 REWARD!
RANAWAY

From the undersigned, living on Current
River, about twelve miles above Doniphan,
in Ripley County, Mo., on 2nd of March, 1860, A NE-
GRO MAN, about 30 years old, weighs about
160 pounds; high forehead, with a scar on it; had on brown pants and coat
very much worn, and an old black wool hat; shoes size No. 11.

The above reward will be given to any person who may apprehend this
said negro out of the State; and fifty dollars if apprehended in this State outside of Ripley county, or $25 if taken in Ripley county.

APOS TUCKER.

Slave owners often
used posters such as
this in an effort to
capture escaped slaves.

In Her Words

Slaves tried to escape from slavery in many ways. Below, for example, slaves escape through a swamp. Harriet described how escaping slaves looked to her during the Combahee Raid: "I never saw such a sight . . . Here you'd see a woman with a pail on her head, rice a-smoking in it just as she'd taken it from the fire, young one hanging on behind, one hand around her forehead to hold on, the other hand digging into the rice pot, eating with all its might . . . bags on their shoulders, baskets on their heads . . . pigs squealing, chickens screaming, young ones squealing."

Chapter Two

A Childhood in Slavery

Around 1820, a baby girl was born to slave parents in Dorchester County, Maryland. The parents worked on a plantation, a large farm that often grows just one crop such as cotton. They named their daughter Araminta Ross. People on the plantation called her Minty. Later, her name was changed to Harriet. She was the property of plantation owner Edward Brodas.

When Harriet was 5 years old, Brodas rented her to the Cook family. Harriet's job was to wind yarn. At night, she slept on the kitchen floor. She shared table scraps with the dogs. Harriet became ill while working barefoot during the winter. The Cooks sent her back to Brodas, and Harriet's mother cared for her until she was well.

When Harriet was 7, Brodas rented her to another home. There, she was to clean house and

A plantation like the one in the top illustration was where
Harriet Tubman was born in Dorchester County, Maryland.
Cotton (small photo) was a common crop on many plantations.

take care of a baby. Harriet had never learned how to clean a house. Many nights, she had to stay up rocking the baby. Her owner's wife whipped her hard and often. One day, Harriet stole a sugarcube from the kitchen. As punishment, the owner beat her and sent her home. Again, her mother fed her and tended her wounds.

Brodas decided that Harriet should no longer work indoors. He sent her outdoors to split fence rails and load wood onto wagons. Harriet was small but strong, and she preferred to work outdoors.

A Blow to the Head

When Harriet was about 15, she watched a young slave named Jim slip away. He went to a store in town without permission. Harriet followed Jim. The man in charge of the slaves, called the overseer, followed Jim, too. Cornering Jim, the overseer asked Harriet to help tie him up. Harriet refused, and Jim ran out the door.

The overseer picked up a 2-pound (1-kilogram) weight from a scale. He threw the weight at Jim. It missed Jim but hit Harriet in the head. She fell to the floor, knocked out.

Nat Turner's Rebellion

Some of Harriet's ideas about freeing slaves may have come from stories about Nat Turner, shown below being captured. Occasionally, slaves would rebel, fighting for their freedom from slavery. In 1831, Turner led a rebellion not far from where 11-year-old Harriet lived. Turner and a group of escaped slaves killed more than 50 white people. Turner and his group were caught and put to death. Harriet had probably heard about this rebellion.

Food of Slavery

Slaves did not eat the rich diet their owners enjoyed. They often received a set amount of cornmeal once a year. The women mixed the meal with water and laid the mixture between leaves to bake in a fire. Field workers brought these "ashcakes" to the fields. The cakes were their main meal of the day. Children ate cornmeal mush together from a single bowl, using clamshells as spoons.

Every year, each family was given a pig. To add to the diet, the slaves might trap wild game or keep a garden.

For several months, Harriet lay near death, but her mother nursed her. As Harriet healed, she began to appreciate religion. For the rest of her life, Harriet depended on God to guide and help her. During her life as a slave and later as a free woman, Harriet prayed and thought about ways to help her people escape.

Harriet's injury left a dent in her forehead. Though Harriet returned to hard labor, her injury caused her to fall suddenly asleep several times a day. These blackouts continued for the rest of her life.

Harriet as a Young Woman

Finally, Harriet was hired out to someone who did not beat her. This person was John Stewart, a local builder. At first, he wanted her to do housework. Harriet preferred to work outdoors. Though she was only 5 feet (1.5 meters) tall, people throughout the county noticed Harriet's unusual strength. Soon, she was cutting down trees with the men.

After several years, Stewart allowed Harriet to buy the right to work for herself. She paid Stewart $50 per year. In return, he let Harriet keep money she earned working in her spare time. Each day after finishing her work for Stewart, Harriet hauled wood to earn money. She bought an ox and started to keep a vegetable garden.

In 1844, Harriet married a free African American named John Tubman, who was a tailor. Harriet's hard work probably impressed him. She wanted to escape to the North, but John was not interested in leaving. He did not even want Harriet to talk about escaping.

Not all slave families were lucky enough to be able to keep a vegetable garden. But slaves like Harriet who did keep a garden could grow extra food to sell.

Nightmares and Dreams

Harriet had nightmares of being sold south. Being sold would mean a more difficult life picking cotton. It would also make escape harder. Two of Harriet's sisters had already been sold south. Several times Harriet heard that she might be sold, too.

Harriet dreamed of escape. She lived only 90 miles (145 kilometers) from Pennsylvania, a state where slavery was illegal. In her dreams, Harriet could fly like a bird. Ladies in white would help her if she stumbled or wanted to give up. Harriet often heard voices. They warned her to run for her life.

Harriet's Escape

In 1849, Harriet's nightmare seemed to be coming true. Another slave warned Harriet that she was to be sold the next day. Harriet decided to escape the night before being sold.

Harriet visited the plantation where her parents lived. She wanted them to know where she was going. It was too dangerous for Harriet to speak to them directly. Some people believe that Harriet walked past her parents while singing a Negro

spiritual song. The song's words told her family
what she was going to do.

I'll meet you in the morning,
When I reach the Promised Land,
On the other side of Jordan
for I'm bound for the Promised Land.

That night, Harriet left without a word to
anyone, not even her husband. She went to the home of
a Quaker woman in a nearby town. Quakers belong
to the Religious Society of Friends. Quakers'
religious faith teaches them that slavery is wrong
and that they should help people escape it. Harriet
had learned that this woman helped runaway slaves.

The woman's home was on the Underground
Railroad. This escape route was a series of safe
houses. The people who owned them helped
runaway slaves escape to freedom. The Quaker
woman sent Harriet to the next stop on the railroad.

Harriet eventually arrived in Philadelphia.
She heard about the Pennsylvania Anti-Slavery
Society. Its members were abolitionists. They
worked to outlaw slavery. Many of the society's
members were conductors on the Underground

Abolitionists

When Harriet escaped from slavery, the abolitionist movement was in full force. The first antislavery newspapers were published in the 1830s, when Harriet was about 10. Frederick Douglass (right), a former slave, printed a newspaper called the *North Star*. William Lloyd Garrison of Boston published *The Liberator*. Articles in the papers persuaded others to oppose slavery. By the time Harriet escaped, all of the Northern states had abolished slavery. More than 200,000 Americans belonged to 2,000 antislavery organizations.

Railroad. These people, often former slaves, helped slaves escape from the South. Harriet decided to become a conductor.

Harriet found a job in the kitchen of a hotel. As soon as she had saved enough money, Harriet planned to rescue her sister, Mary Ann Bowley.

Chapter Three

Moses of the Underground Railroad

Harriet's sister, Mary Ann, was married to John Bowley, a free man. To contact her sister, Harriet sent a letter to John. Harriet could not read or write, so she may have had someone write the letter for her. Harriet's letter suggested that John bring his family to Baltimore, Maryland. Harriet would bring them the rest of the way to freedom.

Before the letter arrived, Mary Ann's owner unexpectedly sold her. John rescued her and took her and their children by boat to Baltimore. Harriet met them and helped them to Philadelphia. Harriet's first rescue was a success.

In 1850, Harriet returned to Dorchester County and rescued her brother, John. That fall, she went again to ask her husband, John Tubman, to come with her. John still was not interested in going North.

This picture shows how Philadelphia looked in Harriet's lifetime.
She lived in the city when she first escaped from slavery.

The Fugitive Slave Act

Congress passed the Fugitive Slave Act in 1850.
This law made it easier for escaped slaves in the
North to be returned to their Southern owners. The
law resulted from arguments between the North and
the South. The two sides argued whether new
territories should allow slavery. A territory is land
that is a part of the United States but not yet a
state. The sides reached an agreement. Northern
states accepted the Fugitive Slave Act in exchange
for California being declared a free state.

Harriet felt that the slaves she helped were no
longer safe even in the North. She started taking
them to Canada. Slavery was illegal in the entire
country. She took slaves to St. Catharines, a small
Canadian town on the southern tip of Lake Ontario.
Instead of 90 miles (145 kilometers), Harriet took
freed slaves more than 500 miles (805 kilometers).

How She Did It

Harriet usually picked up her passengers on
Saturday night. Their owner probably would not
miss them on Sunday, a slave's day off. Harriet took

Did You Know?

Although Delaware was a slave state, only about one in 10 African Americans living there was a slave. Harriet probably led her people through Delaware because it was easier for an escaped slave to hide there. Slave catchers (below) had a harder time deciding who were slaves and who were free African Americans.

groups of five to seven people. She helped men, women, and children escape.

Harriet did not use the same route every time. She often followed the Choptank River from Maryland to Delaware. Sometimes she took a ferry or boat. People on the Underground Railroad might offer her a horse and wagon to use. She also took trains, especially in New York. To fool slave catchers, Harriet might get on a train going south. Few slave catchers thought an escaping slave would be foolish

Did You Know?

Riding a train was dangerous for runaway slaves. Many train workers wanted the reward money that was offered for capturing runaways. Some workers weighed and measured each African American. They compared that person's appearance to information on wanted posters to see if it matched.

enough to travel toward slavery. When it was safe, Harriet would get on another train heading north.

On the Way to Freedom

Many people helped Harriet. She and her runaway slaves often visited Thomas Garrett in Wilmington, Delaware. Garrett had a shoe factory. No one left his home without new shoes. In Philadelphia, Harriet and her group stayed with William Still, a former slave who had become a leader in the Underground Railroad.

William Seward, a U.S. senator, helped Harriet in Auburn, New York. In later years, Harriet bought a house there with Seward's help. Seward went on to become governor of New York state.

From 1850 to 1860, Harriet made 19 trips into slave territory. She brought 300 slaves to freedom, including her elderly parents. Slave owners posted rewards for her capture. As she became famous, more money was offered. At times, the South swarmed with slave catchers, yet Harriet was never caught and never lost a passenger.

Harriet was an excellent leader who could think her way to safety. Once, she hid a group of escaping slaves in a heap of animal waste. The runaways breathed through straws until it was safe to leave.

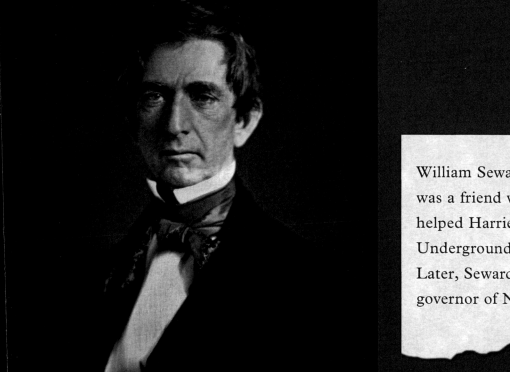

William Seward (left) was a friend who helped Harriet and the Underground Railroad. Later, Seward became governor of New York.

The Moses of Her People

Harriet believed God guided her. Once, Harriet heard a voice that told her to cross a river. She did not question the voice, which she thought belonged to God. She and her passengers quickly plunged into the river, though it was icy. The water was neck high, but everyone reached the far side. Later, Harriet learned that slave catchers had set a trap for her on the other side. If she had not obeyed the voice, Harriet and her group probably would have been caught.

The house at right was one of many houses along the Underground Railroad. Escaping slaves could get help at these houses.

Sometimes escaping slaves became frightened and wanted to turn back. Harriet would not allow it. She carried a gun with her. Once, she threatened a passenger, "Brother, you go on or die." She did not want anyone leaving the group and putting other people's lives in danger.

To give her passengers courage, Harriet sang spirituals. One of her favorite songs was about Moses. The Bible tells how Moses led his people from slavery. Some of the song's words say,

> *Oh go down, Moses*
> *Way down in Egypt land,*
> *Tell old Pharaoh*
> *To let my people go.*

Soon most slaves and many Northerners called Harriet "Moses." Southern slaves waited for their Moses to rescue them. Slave catchers worked hard to capture her.

In the North, Harriet began speaking at abolitionist meetings. Many abolitionists wanted to work with this successful woman.

Chapter Four

Work in the Civil War

John Brown was an abolitionist who believed that only a war would free the slaves. He met with Harriet for help on a plan. In 1859, Brown and his men attacked Harpers Ferry, a small town in Virginia. They took over part of the arsenal, where the U.S. government kept weapons. Many of Brown's group were killed, and Brown was hanged.

Harriet had planned to be at Harpers Ferry, too, but she was ill and could not go. If Harriet had been with Brown, she might have been killed, too.

Harriet respected Brown. After his death, she often called him "the saviour of our people." When Harriet's name was found among Brown's papers, her friends took her to Canada. They believed she would not be safe anywhere in the United States.

In 1860, Abraham Lincoln became U.S. president. Lincoln hated slavery. Many Southern states threatened to secede from, or leave, the Union if he were elected.

John Brown and his group captured this building, part of the arsenal at Harpers Ferry, Virginia. Brown hoped to free Southern slaves by giving them weapons from the storehouse and encouraging armed resistance.

The North and South in 1861

When the U.S. Civil War began, 23 states belonged to the Union. The Confederacy had 11 states.

Before Lincoln took office, South Carolina and six other states had seceded from the United States. These states called themselves the Confederate States of America. Later, four more Southern states joined them.

Lincoln did not want war. He tried to work with the Southern states. He promised not to stop slavery in the South. Lincoln believed that slavery would end on its own.

Lincoln, however, did not believe that any state had the right to secede from, or leave, the Union. He did not want a war but was willing to fight one to stop the Southern states from seceding.

The Civil War Begins

A battle at Fort Sumter, South Carolina, began the Civil War. Supplies at the fort were running out for Union, or Northern, troops. The Confederates hoped the troops would leave when the food ran out, so the South could take over the fort. But Lincoln tried to send the troops supplies. After many hours, the Confederates won the battle for the fort.

Helping Freed Slaves

Once the war began, Harriet followed the Union Army into Maryland, a place she knew well. Many slaves found freedom with the Union troops, and Harriet was there to help them.

Slaves hid for weeks in some places and then risked their lives to reach Union troops. These runaways needed help learning to live as free people. The Union Army in South Carolina asked for volunteers to help the runaways. Harriet went at once to help.

Harriet helped feed and clothe the escaped slaves. She also treated their diseases with herbs, such as those below. To earn money, Harriet started a laundry. African American women washed and mended clothes for Union soldiers. The money the women earned went to help the freed slaves.

At first, the Union gave Harriet food rations for her help. But the freed slaves did not understand why she was getting food when they were not. They had never heard of Harriet Tubman. So Harriet gave up her rations.

In Her Own Words

The painting below shows a Union Army officer calming a group of angry white Southerners (left) and former slaves (right) at a Freedman's Bureau. The bureaus helped freed slaves adjust to their life after slavery. Harriet wrote about former slaves:

"Most of those [former slaves] coming are very destitute [poor], almost naked. I am trying to find places for those able to work, and provide for them as best I can . . . while at the same time they learn to respect themselves by earning their own living."

Nursing the Wounded

Harriet described part of her work in the Union hospitals such as the one shown below:

"I'd go to the hospital early every morning. I'd get a big chunk of ice and put it in a basin and fill it with water; then I'd take a sponge and begin. First man I'd come to, I'd thrash away the flies, and they'd rise, like bees around a hive. Then I'd begin to bathe the wounds, and by the time I'd bathed off three or four, the fire and heat would have melted the ice and made the water warm, and it would be as red as clear blood. Then I'd go and get more ice."

Harriet made gingerbread, pies, and root beer at night. She then hired African Americans to sell the food to the soldiers.

Nurse Harriet

Harriet also worked as a nurse in Union hospitals. She was willing to do anything to help, including scrubbing and cleaning.

Once, Harriet was sent to Florida to help soldiers dying of dysentery. This disease causes severe diarrhea, or frequent, runny human waste. Dysentery usually occurs in unclean conditions. Harriet had gained a reputation for being able to cure dysentery with roots of certain plants. She also treated soldiers for smallpox and other fevers but never got sick herself.

Harriet was sent to other battle areas, such as Fort Wagner, South Carolina. At the battle, African American soldiers fought for the first time. From a hill, Harriet watched the terrible fighting. Most of the men were killed. Harriet nursed the few wounded soldiers. She then helped to bury the dead.

Did You Know?

Twice as many Civil War soldiers died from diseases as from war injuries.

Harriet the Spy

Union leaders believed that Harriet's Underground Railroad experiences had prepared her to be a good spy. The leaders asked Harriet from time to time to leave her nursing duties to gather information in enemy territory. Harriet would pretend to be a slave. She could easily cross enemy lines because most people ignored a female slave. Then, Harriet watched the land and spoke to slaves. In this way, she gathered valuable information that helped the Union Army.

In 1862, Harriet was put in charge of organizing a group of scouts and spies. As scouts, she chose nine African American men who knew the land well. These men helped Harriet prepare for the Combahee Raid. They reported that many slaves on plantations along the river were waiting to be freed. They also knew that the Confederacy had placed bombs in the river.

In 1863, Union leaders asked Harriet to lead the raid on the Combahee River. It was the first of many raids in which Harriet and her scouts participated. This first raid was a complete success.

On January 1, 1863, President Lincoln issued the Emancipation Proclamation. The proclamation was an order to free slaves in Confederate-held areas.

The War Ends

By 1864, Harriet needed to rest. She left for Auburn, New York, to visit her elderly parents.

In April 1865, Harriet's dreams came true when the Union won the Civil War. The Southern states returned to the Union.

In December 1865, Congress passed the 13th Amendment to the U.S. Constitution. The amendment outlawed slavery in the United States. The 14th Amendment, passed in 1868, granted U.S. citizenship to all former slaves.

Harriet and other African Americans still faced many problems including racial injustice. On the train to Auburn after the war, Harriet had a pass that entitled her to pay only half price. The conductor, however, did not believe that she was an army nurse. He and two other men forced Harriet into the baggage car. During the struggle, the men twisted her arm. It was years before she recovered from this first war-related injury.

Bloomers for Harriet

Harriet wrote that during the Combahee Raid, she stepped on her dress "and fell and tore it almost off, so that when I got on board the boat, there was hardly anything left of it but shreds. I made up my mind then I would never wear a long dress on another expedition . . . but would have a bloomer as soon as I could get it."

The bloomer dress (shown at left) was named after its creator, Amelia Bloomer. It consisted of loose pants worn under a short skirt. Bloomers made it easier for women to move around actively. Newspaper writers and other people disapproved of bloomers, believing that women should not wear pants. However, many women's rights activists wore them. Soon after Harriet wrote the letter, someone sent her a pair of bloomers.

Chapter Five

Final Years

Harriet spent the last years of her life in her house in Auburn. After many hardships, Harriet wanted to rest.

But many former slaves still needed help and found their way to Harriet's doorstep. They believed that the famous Harriet Tubman would help them. Soon Harriet was taking care of a group of sick and aging former slaves. She kept a large vegetable garden and sold vegetables and chickens door to door. Harriet also asked friends for help. She raised enough money to support two schools for freed slaves in the South.

After the war, Harriet was busy. She spoke at suffrage meetings. Suffragists worked for women's right to vote. She also supported the temperance movement. People in this movement worked to get people to stop drinking alcohol. And she helped to build the African Methodist Episcopal Church in Philadelphia.

Harriet spent the last years of her life in this house in
Auburn, New York.

Reaching the End

Harriet wanted to be named a Civil War veteran so she could collect a government pension. A person receives pension money after retiring from a job. Several well-known people tried to help Harriet be named a war veteran. Newspapers published articles of support. Twice, Congress introduced laws that would provide Harriet with a pension. Nothing came of these efforts, and Harriet continued to be poor.

Harriet married Nelson Davis in 1869. Davis had been a Union soldier during the Civil War whom Harriet had met in South Carolina. He was 20 years younger than Harriet. Davis died in 1888 of a lung disease when Harriet was 68. As the widow of a Civil War veteran, Harriet finally was able to collect a pension of $20 a month.

In 1908, with money she saved from the pension, Harriet bought 25 acres (10 hectares) of land next to her house. She turned the land into a farm that African Americans operated. Harriet also started a home for the disabled and aged, where she herself later received care.

Harriet became ill with pneumonia. She died
of the illness on March 10, 1913, at age 93. Her
death made international newspaper headlines. She
was buried with full military honors.

This photo shows
Harriet in 1910, a few
years before her death
at age 93.

TIMELINE

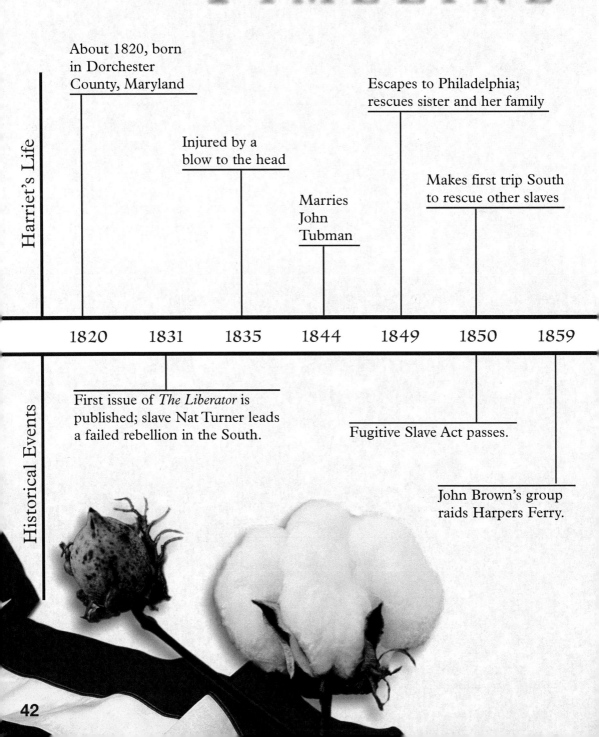

Harriet's Life

About 1820, born in Dorchester County, Maryland

Injured by a blow to the head

Marries John Tubman

Escapes to Philadelphia; rescues sister and her family

Makes first trip South to rescue other slaves

| 1820 | 1831 | 1835 | 1844 | 1849 | 1850 | 1859 |

Historical Events

First issue of *The Liberator* is published; slave Nat Turner leads a failed rebellion in the South.

Fugitive Slave Act passes.

John Brown's group raids Harpers Ferry.

Dies in Auburn, New York

Marries Nelson Davis

Last trip as conductor of the Underground Railroad

Builds home for the sick and elderly in Auburn, New York

Begins work for the Union Army in the Civil War

| 1860 | 1861 | 1863 | 1865 | 1868 | 1869 | 1908 | 1913 |

Emancipation Proclamation; Combahee Raid.

The 14th Amendment makes African Americans U.S. citizens.

U.S. Civil War begins.

Lincoln elected president; South Carolina secedes from Union.

Civil War ends; 13th Amendment outlaws slavery.

Glossary

abolitionist (ab-uh-LISH-uh-nist)—a person who works to end slavery

civil war (SIV-il WOR)—a conflict between different groups of people within the same country; the North and South fought the U.S. Civil War.

conductor (kuhn-DUHK-tur)—a person who led runaway slaves to the North on the Underground Railroad

Emancipation Proclamation (i-man-si-PAY-shun prok-luh-MAY-shuhn)—Abraham Lincoln's written order to free the slaves in Confederate-held areas

fugitive (FYOO-juh-tiv)—someone who is running away, especially from the law

overseer (OH-vur-seer)—someone paid to watch over slaves

pension (PEN-shuhn)—money regularly paid to a person after retirement

plantation (plan-TAY-shuhn)—a large farm where usually a single main crop is grown

secede (si-SEED)—to leave one group to form another group

slave (SLAYV)—a person who is owned by someone else

Underground Railroad (UHN-dur-ground RAYL-rohd)—a group of safe houses and people who helped runaway slaves

For Further Reading

Bradford, Sarah. *Harriet Tubman: The Moses of Her People.* Bedford, Mass.: Applewood Books, 1993. First published in 1869.

Lutz, Norma Jean. *Harriet Tubman: Leader of the Underground Railroad.* Famous Figures of the Civil War Era. Philadelphia: Chelsea House, 2000.

Roehm, Michelle. *Girls Who Rocked the World 2: Heroines from Harriet Tubman to Mia Hamm.* Hillsboro, Ore.: Beyond Words, 2000.

Sullivan, George. *Harriet Tubman.* In Their Own Words. New York: Scholastic, 2001.

Places of Interest

African Methodist Episcopal Church
Sixth and Lombard Streets
Philadelphia, Pennsylvania
Center for the temperance
movement, which
Harriet supported

Anacostia Museum
1901 Fort Place SE
Washington, DC 20020
http://www.si.edu/anacostia
Museum of African American
history and culture

Appoquinimink Friends Meeting House
Main Street
(Route 299)
Odessa, DE 19730
Meetinghouse of Harriet's Quaker
friends in Delaware

The Harriet Tubman Home
180 South Street
Auburn, NY 13021
Harriet's home near the end of
her life

Johnson House
6306 Germantown Avenue
Germantown, PA 19144
1850s safe house on the
Underground Railroad

St. Catharines British Methodist Episcopal Church (Salem Chapel)
92 Geneva Street
ON L2R 4N2
Canada
*http://parkscanada.pch.gc.ca/
library/background/179_e.htm*
Traditional house of worship for
Harriet and other escaped slaves

Internet Sites

Do you want to learn more about Harriet Tubman?
Visit the FactHound at *www.facthound.com*

FactHound can track down many sites to help you. All the
FactHound sites are hand-selected by our editors. FactHound will
fetch the best, most accurate information to answer your questions.

IT'S EASY! IT'S FUN!
1) Go to *www.facthound.com*
2) Type in: **0736810870**
3) Click on **FETCH IT** and FactHound will put you on the trail
   of several helpful links.

You can also search by subject or book title. So, relax
and let our pal FactHound do the research for you!

Index